SOHRAB AND RUSTUM

AN EPISODE

BY

MATTHEW ARNOLD

WILDSIDE PRESS

INTRODUCTION.

MATTHEW ARNOLD was born at Laleham, England, Dec. 24, 1822. He was the son of Dr. Thomas Arnold, who, as head master of the Rugby School, was accounted one of the greatest educational reformers of England.

Matthew Arnold entered Rugby in 1837, and a few years later went to Balliol College, Oxford, where in 1840 he won a scholarship for proficiency in Latin. In 1843 he won the Newdigate prize for English verse, the subject of his poem being "Cromwell."

While Arnold was a student at Oxford, he associated with such men as Thomas Hughes, the Froudes, Bishop Fraser, Dean Church, John Henry Newman, and Arthur Hugh Clough. With Clough he formed a deep friendship, and mourned his death in the exquisite elegiac poem "Thyrsis." In 1844 he was graduated with honors, and in 1845 was elected a fellow of Oriel College. Two years later he became private secretary to Lord Lansdowne, which position he held until 1851.

Up to this date Arnold's life had been preëminently that of a student, although in 1848 he had published his first volume of song, "The Strayed Reveler, and other Poems," and later the narrative poem, "The Sick King in Bokhara." But in 1851, after a short term as assistant teacher at Rugby, he was appointed lay inspector of schools, under the Committee of Council on Education, and began his valuable and efficient work in educational matters which formed the regular occupation of his life. The same year he married the daughter of Justice Wightman.

In 1859 he visited France, Germany, and Holland, to inquire into the methods of primary education in those countries; and he published his observations on this subject in 1868, in an essay entitled "Schools and Universities on the Continent." In 1865 he again went abroad, this time with the view of reporting on the schools for the middle and upper classes in France and Germany; and shortly before retiring from the office of inspector, he made a third journey to the Continent, and examined particularly the elementary schools of the different nations.

It was only a few years before his death that he resigned (1886) his position under the Committee of Council on Education. He was at all times an ardent advocate of soundness and excellence in elementary education; and his observation soon led him to attribute to the lack of organized middle-class education the dullness, sordid instincts, blind prejudices, and moral obtuseness that characterize the middle classes of English society. Grouping these faults under the name "Philistinism," he held them up for reprobation, and labored to prove that they could be remedied only by better and broader education.

In 1853 Arnold published "Empedocles, and other Poems; " but he soon became dissatisfied with much in the volume, and suppressed the whole work. Yet this book, in addition to the former volumes of verse, established his reputation as a poet in England; and in 1857 he was elected professor of poetry at Oxford, a chair which he held for ten years. "Merope," a tragedy, with a volume entitled "New Poems," published in 1869, finishes the list of his poetical works.

A series of essays on translating Homer was published in 1861, and was followed in 1868 by another on the study of Celtic literature. His great and enduring work, however, appeared in 1865, and consisted of two series of prose discourses, "Essays in Criticism." The treatises "Culture and Anarchy," and "Irish Essays and others," followed.

The modern tendency to drift away from the old established religious faith was a source of serious grief, and matter for deep thought, to Arnold. He gave his mind to the consideration of what was best and most lasting in religion, and tried to give to the world a rational creed that would satisfy the skeptics and attract the indifferent. The volumes "St. Paul and Protestantism" (1871), "Literature and Dogma" (1873), "God and the Bible" (1875), and "Last Essays on Church and State" (1877), embody the fruit of his thought in this direction.

Arnold delivered the Cambridge Annual Rede Lecture in June, 1882, choosing for his subject "Literature and Science." He received the degree of LL.D. from Edinburgh in 1869, and from his own college, Oxford, in 1870.

He visited the United States twice. The first time he delivered a lecture on Emerson, and one on the principle and value of numbers. During his second visit, in 1886, made for the Committee of Council on Education, he delivered a lecture on the subject of education on the European continent. Arnold was struck by the relative lack of ideality, absence of great institutions, and predominance of the money-getting mania in America. His criticism of our nation, though perhaps just, was severe; but it was no more severe than were many of his criticisms of English traits and of the institutions of his native land.

He died suddenly and quietly of heart disease, at the house of a friend in Liverpool, England, on April 15, 1888. He was buried at his birthplace, Laleham. By his death England lost a learned scholar, a polished writer, an earnest educational reformer, a good man, and, above all, one of her most acute and cultured critics.

Matthew Arnold was deeply imbued with the spirit of Greek culture, and in this culture he found his ideal standards, to which he brought for comparison all questions that engrossed his thoughts. He is perhaps the purest classic writer that England ever produced; classic not merely in the repose of his style, but in the unity and simplicity of his habit of thought.

Mr. Jacobs, in the " Athenæum," gives a very just criticism of Arnold, from which the substance of the following is taken.

Although it is quite usual to speak of Arnold as having revolutionized English book criticism, when we come to examine the facts, we realize that his judgments of books were few, and were not always trustworthy. He criticised authors and their work in a general way, rather than any of their books in particular.

But why, then, we ask, was Matthew Arnold such a force in criticism, and where did he gain his reputation as a critic?

" What he did in criticism was to introduce the *causerie* (or chat), and with it the personal element. The personality of Matthew Arnold was, with all its affectations and mannerisms, so attractive, that a chat with him charmed not so much by adding to our information about the author or his books, as because it added to our knowledge of Matthew Arnold."

His was a criticism of life, and dealt with the deepest issues of his time: he discussed problems social, theological, and literary. His exposition was rather peculiar. He recognized the fact that iteration and reiteration of certain formulæ would impress on the mind the particular view which they were designed to express. This repetition may have been exasperating, but it effected its purpose, as we cannot fail to see when we recall some of these phrases, as " sweetness and light," "criticism of life," " barbarians, Philistines, and populace," " the need of expression, the need of manners, the need of intellect, the need of beauty, the need of conduct." While the effect of these formulæ may have been chiefly mechanical, the discussions which they summarized were examples of the most logical inductive or deductive reasoning.

His powers of analysis were great, and his summary of "needs" given above is a remarkable description of man as a social being. He gave the vogue to the cultus of culture, which was in his hands something precise. Although civilization is a difficult problem to analyze, yet, when he spoke of it, it seemed to be something real and definite, and not the vague abstractions of the sophist.

His power of analysis showed itself clearly in his theological studies. As regards his own solution of the religious problem, little need here be said. His very formula, which is purposely vague and indefinite, is its own condemnation; but it must not be forgotten that his literary tone, and the gentle irony with which he treated all extremes, helped to prevent an explosion of theological or anti-theological polemics. Although his particular way of putting his solution of theological difficulties is not likely to gain many disciples, he has certainly greatly influenced English opinion; and we may feel that he was right in laying stress upon his theological activity and its results, as the most influential and abiding part of his work.

Arnold began life as a poet, and, if we can divorce the poet from the technique of his art, he remained one to the end.   His was a poetic force, a uniform recognition of the permanent power and reality of the ideal element in the human character. He himself has defined his ideas of poetry, and they are seen to be distinctly Greek.   He says, " The radical difference between the poetic theory of the Greeks and our own is this : that with them the poetical character of the action in itself, and the con- duct of it, was the first consideration ; with us, attention is fixed mainly on the value of the separate thoughts and images which occur in the treatment of an action.   They regarded the whole : we regard the parts.   We have poems which seem to exist merely for the sake of single lines and passages, and not for the sake of producing any total impression.   We have critics who seem to direct their attention merely to detached expressions, to the lan- guage about the action, not to the action itself.   I verily believe that the majority of them do not believe that there is such a thing as a total impression to be derived from a poem at all, or to be demanded from a poet.   They will permit the poet to select any action he pleases, and to suffer that action to go as it will, pro- vided he gratifies them with occasional bursts of fine writing, and with a shower of isolated thoughts and images ; that is, they per- mit him to leave their poetical sense ungratified, provided that he gratifies their rhetorical sense and their curiosity."

He has illustrated with remarkable success his ideas of that unity which gratifies the poetical sense, and has approached very close to his Greek models in his epic or narrative poem of " Sohrab and Rustum."   Here we have a theme which is in- tensely tragic, and which challenges our sympathy at once.   A young hero in search of his warrior father, whom he has never seen, meets him in deadly single combat between the lines of contending armies; but it is only after he has received a mortal wound by his father's hand, that the relationship is discovered. The accessories are in keeping with the wildness of the main incident. The weird shapes of the Tartar hordes and of the Iranian hosts, awaiting the event of the combat, are dimly seen on the edge of the desert through the mists of the Oxus; while, in sharp contrast with the passions and anguish awakened in the tragedy enacted on its banks, the mighty river maintains its calm and majestic flow out "into the frosty starlight," and typifies the inexorableness of fate. The treatment, in smooth and simple verse, is strictly subordinated and adapted to the action of the theme, and the whole is admirably calculated to impart that totality of impression which Mr. Arnold and the Greeks esteemed so highly. It has been said of this poem that it is "the nearest analogue in English to the rapidity of action, plainness of thought, plainness of diction, and nobleness of Homer."

The episode of "Sohrab and Rustum" is found in the great Persian epic poem called the "Shah Nameh," which was composed by the native poet Firdusi towards the end of the tenth century. This poem is to Persian literature about what the Iliad and the Odyssey are to the Greek, and purports to comprise the annals and achievements of the ancient Persian kings from Kaiumers to the conquest of the Empire by the Saracens in 636,—an estimated period of thirty-six centuries. It was gathered from the tales and legends traditionally known throughout the country, and abounds in adventures of the most wild and romantic description. The principal hero of the poem is Rustum, a prodigy of strength, piety, and valor, who, during his career of several centuries, and mounted on his famous horse Ruksh, is the bulwark of the Persian throne; in its defense slaying countless enemies, overcoming devouring monsters, circumventing magicians, and overthrowing works of enchantment. Of all the adventures of the mighty Rustum, the most dramatic is the conflict with his son Sohrab. This forms but an episode in the complete story of Sohrab and Rustum, an outline of which is as follows: —

Rustum, having killed a wild ass while hunting on the borders of Turan and having partaken of its flesh, composed himself to sleep, leaving his horse Ruksh to graze at liberty. When he awoke, his favorite steed had disappeared, and, feeling convinced that it had been stolen, he hastened towards Samengan, a neighboring city, in which direction the hoof-prints led him. Upon encountering the King of Samengan he wrathfully demanded his stolen property; but the ruler met him so hospitably, and offered such cordial help in searching for the missing horse, that Rustum was appeased, and finally accompanied the King to the royal palace. There he met the beautiful princess Tahmineh, who had become enamored of him on account of his bravery and famous deeds. She informed him that she had stolen Ruksh in the hope of leading Rustum to her father's court, and winning him for a husband. She proposed that he should ask her father's consent to their union. To this Rustum agreed, and they were married with great pomp. Rustum was obliged to leave his bride soon thereafter, and at parting gave her an amulet, saying, " If the Almighty should bless our union with a daughter, place this amulet in her hair; but if a son, bind it on his arm, and it will inspire him with great valor." Having regained his horse Ruksh, he left Samengan. The fruit of this union was a marvelous son, whom the King called Sohrab. Tahmineh, fearing Rustum would take the boy from her, sent word that the child was a girl, and thereupon Rustum took no more interest in it.

When Sohrab was about ten years old, he demanded his father's name, and, upon hearing that it was the warrior Rustum, he determined to go in search of him. His mother's entreaties that he would keep his parentage a secret availed nothing, and at parting Tahmineh bound on Sohrab's arm the amulet which Rustum had given her.

The news that Sohrab was about to wage war with Persia in order to gain that kingdom for his father mightily pleased Afrasiab, King of the Turanians, who desired the overthrow of King Kaoos for purposes of his own.

He accordingly sent to the youth's assistance an army commanded by Haman, instructing that chief to keep the knowledge of their relationship from both father and son. The army proceeded, and on the way Sohrab overthrew the Persian Hujir, and then conquered the warrior maiden Gurdafrid, but, moved by her beauty and her entreaties, released her. She hastened to the court of Kaoos to warn him of the coming of the youthful Sohrab, who would overthrow the Persian power. Kaoos, in great terror, sent a messenger to call Rustum to his aid. Regardless of the King's urgent demands, Rustum spent eight days in feasting, and then departed for the Persian court. Kaoos, in wrath at the delay thus caused, ordered both Rustum and the messenger to be put to death; but the former, after reproaching the King for his ingratitude, escaped on his horse Ruksh.

When the King's anger had cooled, he recognized the danger of his throne if unsupported by Rustum's prowess, and sent for the chief with many apologies. Rustum was finally prevailed upon to return, and advanced at the head of the Persians to resist the opposing army.

The morning before the opening of hostilities, Sohrab took the captive Hujir to the top of the fortress, and asked him which was Rustum's tent; but Hujir, fearing that Sohrab would attack the Persian when the latter was unprepared, pretended that Rustum's tent was not among those on the plain. His hopes of finding his father here thus frustrated, Sohrab, armed for battle, descended into the plain, and challenged Kai Kaoos himself. The King sent for Rustum to take up the bold challenge, and the latter was finally persuaded to meet the Tartar champion. When he saw Sohrab, he was moved by his youth and gallant bearing, and counseled him to retire. Sohrab, filled with sudden hope, demanded whether he were Rustum; but the warrior declared that he was only the servant of Rustum, whereupon, disappointed and saddened, Sohrab prepared for battle, and the combat commenced.

They fought with spears, which were soon shivered to pieces, then with swords, clubs, and bows and arrows. Finally Sohrab struck Rustum a heavy blow with a mace, which caused him to reel and fall. A truce was then made for that night, and both warriors retired to their tents. Sohrab, still with a faint hope, inquired of Haman whether his opponent were not the mighty Rustum himself. But the chief, bearing in mind Afrasiab's instructions, declared that he knew Rustum well, and this man was not the one Sohrab sought.

When morning broke, both combatants were ready to renew the struggle. When Sohrab saw Rustum, again an instinctive feeling of affection moved him to propose peace, but Rustum refused. They wrestled, and Sohrab threw Rustum on the plain, and was about to slay him, when Rustum called out, that, according to the Persian custom, it was not proper for a man to kill his opponent until he had thrown him a second time. Sohrab, upon hearing these words, returned the dagger to its sheath, and again father and son parted.

When Rustum had escaped from his enemy, he purified himself with water, and prayed that his former strength might be restored to him. His prayer was granted.

The following day the battle was renewed, and the doubtful contest lasted from morning till evening. At length Rustum gained the advantage over Sohrab, and, fearing the youth might be too strong for him, ended the contest by immediately plunging his dagger into Sohrab's side.

The dying Sohrab warned his conqueror to beware of his father's wrath; for "if thou wert a fish, and sought refuge at the bottom of the ocean," he said, " or a star in the heavens, my father would be revenged on thee for this deed."

The warrior asked the name of Sohrab's father, and upon the youth's answer, " His name is Rustum, and my mother is the daughter of the King of Samengan," Rustum fell senseless to the ground, and, when he recovered, he demanded proofs of Sohrab's story. Sohrab unfastened his mail, and showed the amulet which his mother had bound on his arm. At this unmistakable sign, Rustum was overwhelmed with grief, and would have ended his own life had not Sohrab's earnest pleading prevented him.

When the Persian Army beheld Ruksh riderless, they hastened to the spot where Rustum lay in the dust. He bewailed the cruel fate which had brought father and son so strangely together, but Sohrab beautifully said, " Such is my destiny, such the will of fortune. It was decreed that I should perish by the hand of my father. I came like a flash of lightning, and now I depart like the wind." He then requested that his army might be allowed to return home in peace.

When Sohrab was dead, Rustum burned his tents and all his armor, declaring he would no longer fight against the Turanians. At his petition, Kai Kaoos permitted the Tartar tribes to recross the Oxus unmolested. Rustum carried the body of his son to Seistan, the home of his father, and there it was buried with great honor. When the sad tidings of Sohrab's fate reached his mother, Tahmineh, her grief was most violent and lasting. At the end of a year, worn out with her long sorrowing, she died, and " the mother's spirit joined her child in heaven."

Arnold's poem starts at the point where the two armies are encamped by the Oxus River, and proceeds to Sohrab's challenge of the Persian lords, Rustum's final consent to take it up, and the combat itself, and ends with Sohrab's death and his father's lonely grief.

It will be noticed that Mr. Arnold has modified the story somewhat, in order to increase the rapidity of the action, to round out the episode and make it more complete in itself, and to enhance the dignity of the accessories.

Thus the combat is compressed into a single day, and the weapons are different. Sohrab's motive for his challenge to single combat is not, as in the " Shah Nameh," to awe the Persian hosts into submission by the defeat of their bravest warrior, but to bring his name to the ears of Rustum by the fame of a signal feat of arms. For the amulet by which Sohrab proves his identity, is substituted his father's seal pricked into his arm, which is of course a much surer means of identification.

Again: in Arnold's poem, Sohrab's defeat is not due to superior physical strength on the part of his adversary, but to the emotion caused by hearing the beloved name of his father suddenly shouted; and finally, as an instance of the care with which Mr. Arnold selected his theme, and clothed it even in its remoter parts with fittingly dignified surroundings, it is to be noted that he has taken the episode bodily from the reign of the weak and "brainless monarch" Kaoos, in which it is placed in the "Shah Nameh," and transferred it to that of his glorious grandson Khosroo, who has been identified with Cyrus the Great.

SOHRAB[1] AND RUSTUM.

AN EPISODE.

AND the first gray of morning fill'd the east,
 And the fog rose out of the Oxus[2] stream.
But all the Tartar[3] camp along the stream
Was hush'd, and still the men were plunged in sleep;
Sohrab alone, he slept not; all night long   5
He had lain wakeful, tossing on his bed;
But when the gray dawn stole into his tent,
He rose, and clad himself, and girt his sword,
And took his horseman's cloak, and left his tent,
And went abroad into the cold wet fog,   10
Through the dim camp to Peran-Wisa's[4] tent.
 Through the black Tartar tents he pass'd, which stood
Clustering like beehives on the low flat strand
Of Oxus, where the summer floods o'erflow

---

[1] Sōh'räb.

[2] The great river Amu Daria was called the Oxus by the Greeks and Romans, and the Jihun or Amu by the Arabs and Persians.

[3] " Tartar " is the general name applied to many nomadic tribes of southern Russia and central Asia, and particularly to those inhabiting the drainage basin of the Caspian and Aral Seas.

[4] Pē'rän-Wē'sä. The Turänians are the Scythians of the Greek historians. Turän was separated from Irän, or the Persian Empire, by the Oxus. Peran-Wisa was a Turanian chief, and the commander of King Afrasiab's forces, which included representatives of many Tartar tribes, as indicated in lines 119–134.

15   When the sun melts the snows in high Pamere; [1]
Through the black tents he pass'd, o'er that low strand,
And to a hillock came, a little back
From the stream's brink — the spot where first a boat,
Crossing the stream in summer, scrapes the land.
20   The men of former times had crown'd the top
With a clay fort; but that was fall'n, and now
The Tartars built there Peran-Wisa's tent,
A dome of laths, and o'er it felts were spread.
And Sohrab came there, and went in, and stood
25   Upon the thick piled carpets in the tent,
And found the old man sleeping on his bed
Of rugs and felts, and near him lay his arms.
And Peran-Wisa heard him, though the step
Was dull'd; for he slept light, an old man's sleep;
30   And he rose quickly on one arm, and said : —
"Who art thou ? for it is not yet clear dawn.
Speak ! is there news, or any night alarm ? "
But Sohrab came to the bedside, and said : —
"Thou know'st me, Peran-Wisa ! it is I.
35   The sun is not yet risen, and the foe
Sleep; but I sleep not; all night long I lie
Tossing and wakeful, and I come to thee.
For so did King Afrasiab [2] bid me seek
Thy counsel, and to heed thee as thy son,
40   In Samarcand,[3] before the army march'd ;
And I will tell thee what my heart desires.
Thou know'st if, since from Ader-baijan [4] first
I came among the Tartars and bore arms,

---

[1] Pamir Plateau (locally called the " Roof of the World "), in which the Oxus takes its rise at an elevation of about 16,000 feet.

[2] Af-rä'sĭ-yäb.

[3] A city of Turkistan, east of Bokhara.

[4] Äz-er-bī'yän, the northwestern province of Persia, on the Turanian frontier.

I have still served Afrasiab well, and shown,
At my boy's years, the courage of a man.　　　45
This too thou know'st, that while I still bear on
The conquering Tartar ensigns through the world,
And beat the Persians back on every field,
I seek one man, one man, and one alone —
Rustum, my father; who I hoped should greet,　　50
Should one day greet, upon some well-fought field,
His not unworthy, not inglorious son.
So I long hoped, but him I never find.
Come then, hear now, and grant me what I ask.
Let the two arm ies rest to-day; but I　　55
Will challenge forth the bravest Persian lords
To meet me, man to man; if I prevail,
Rustum will surely hear it; if I fall —
Old man, the dead need no one, claim no kin.
Dim is the rumor of a common[1] fight,　　60
Where host meets host, and many names are sunk;
But of a single combat fame speaks clear."
　　He spoke; and Peran-Wisa took the hand
Of the young man in his, and sigh'd, and said:
　"O Sohrab, an unquiet heart is thine !　　65
Canst thou not rest among the Tartar chiefs,
And share the battle's common chance with us
Who love thee, but must press forever first,
In single fight incurring single risk,
To find a father thou hast never seen ?　　70
That were far best, my son, to stay with us
Unmurmuring; in our tents, while it is war,
And when 'tis truce, then in Afrasiab's towns.
But, if this one desire indeed rules all,
To seek out Rustum — seek him not through fight !　　75
Seek him in peace, and carry to his arms,

---

[1] Common in the sense of general.

O Sohrab, carry an unwounded son !
But far hence seek him, for he is not here.
For now it is not as when I was young,
80   When Rustum was in front of every fray ;
But now he keeps apart, and sits at home,
In Seistan,[1] with Zal,[2] his father old.
Whether that [3] his own mighty strength at last
Feels the abhorr'd approaches of old age,
85   Or in [4] some quarrel with the Persian King.
There go !— Thou wilt not ?   Yet my heart forbodes
Danger or death awaits thee on this field.
Fain would I know thee safe and well, though lost
To us ; fain therefore send thee hence, in peace
90   To seek thy father, not seek single fights
In vain ; — but who can keep the lion's cub
From ravening, and who govern Rustum's son ?
Go, I will grant thee what thy heart desires."
    So said he, and dropp'd Sohrab's hand, and left
95   His bed, and the warm rugs whereon he lay ;
And o'er his chilly limbs his woolen coat
He pass'd, and tied his sandals on his feet,
And threw a white cloak round him, and he took
In his right hand a ruler's staff, no sword ;
100   And on his head he set his sheepskin cap,
Black, glossy, curl'd, the fleece of Kara-Kul ; [5]
And raised the curtain of his tent, and call'd
His herald to his side, and went abroad.

---

[1] Sē-is-tän' is a province in southwestern Afghanistan, bordering on Be-
loochistan and Persia.   The Helmund River flows through it to Lake Ha-
moon or Lake Seistan.   On an island in this lake is a fort called Fort
Rustum.   Hamoon is now rather a morass than a lake ; and Lake Zirrah or
Zurrah, to the southeast, is now nearly dry.   This territory was held by
Rustum's family in appanage from the Persian Kings.
[2] Zäl.   [3] " Whether that," i.e., either because.
[4] Because of.   [5] A noted place of pasturage southwest of Bokhara.

The sun by this had risen, and clear'd the fog
From the broad Oxus and the glittering sands.   105
And from their tents the Tartar horsemen filed
Into the open plain; so Haman [1] bade —
Haman, who next to Peran-Wisa ruled
The host, and still was in his lusty prime.
From their black tents, long files of horse, they stream'd;   110
As when some gray November morn the files,
In marching order spread, of long-neck'd cranes
Stream over Casbin [2] and the southern slopes
Of Elburz, from the Aralian estuaries,
Or some frore [3] Caspian reed bed, southward bound   115
For the warm Persian seaboard — so they stream'd.
The Tartars of the Oxus, the King's guard,
First, with black sheepskin caps and with long spears;
Large men, large steeds; who from Bokhara come
And Khiva, and ferment the milk of mares. [4]   120
Next, the more temperate Toorkmuns of the south,
The Tukas, and the lances of Salore,
And those from Attruck [5] and the Caspian sands;
Light men and on light steeds, who only drink
The acrid milk of camels, and their wells.   125
And then a swarm of wandering horse, who came
From far, and a more doubtful service own'd;
The Tartars of Ferghana, from the banks
Of the Jaxartes, [6] men with scanty beards

[1] Hä′män.

[2] An old city on the Persian Plateau, lying about 100 miles northwest of Teheran. Just to the north of the city rises the Elburz Mountains, which separate the Persian Plateau from the depression containing the Caspian and the Aral Seas.

[3] Frozen (from Anglo-Saxon, *froren*).

[4] Koumiss, an intoxicating drink made from mare's or camel's milk, is the prevailing beverage of many of the Steppe tribes.

[5] A tributary to the southeastern end of the Caspian.

[6] The Jaxartes, Sihon, or Syr Daria, flows from the northern part of the

130   And close-set skullcaps; and those wilder hordes
      Who roam o'er Kipchak [1] and the northern waste,
      Kalmucks and unkempt Kuzzaks,[2] tribes who stray
      Nearest the Pole, and wandering Kirghizzes,
      Who come on shaggy ponies from Pamere;
135   These all filed out from camp into the plain.
      And on the other side the Persians form'd; —
      First a light cloud of horse, Tartars they seem'd,
      The Ilyats of Khorassan; [3] and behind,
      The royal troops of Persia, horse and foot,
140   Marshal'd battalions bright in burnish'd steel.
      But Peran-Wisa with his herald came,
      Threading the Tartar squadrons to the front,
      And with his staff kept back the foremost ranks.
      And when Ferood, who led the Persians, saw
145   That Peran-Wisa kept the Tartars back,
      He took his spear, and to the front he came,
      And check'd his ranks, and fix'd them where they stood.
      And the old Tartar came upon the sand
      Betwixt the silent hosts, and spake, and said: —
150   " Ferood, and ye, Persians and Tartars, hear !
      Let there be truce between the hosts to-day.
      But choose a champion from the Persian lords
      To fight our champion Sohrab, man to man."
         As, in the country, on a morn in June,
155   When the dew glistens on the pearled ears,
      A shiver runs through the deep corn [4] for joy —

Pamir Plateau, through the province of Ferghana, to the northeastern end of
the Aral Sea.
    [1] Kipchak is a Khanate about 70 miles below Khiva, on the Amu Daria,
or Oxus.
    [2] Kuzzaks, Kazaks, or Cossacks (literally " riders ") frequent the Steppes
on the northern border of the Aral depression.
    [3] " The Land of the Sun," a desert province in northeastern Persia.
    [4] This word is used with its European significance of " grain: " it is only
in America that it signifies " maize," or Indian corn.

So, when they heard what Peran-Wisa said,
A thrill through all the Tartar squadrons ran
Of pride and hope for Sohrab, whom they loved.
But as a troop of peddlers, from Cabool,   160
Cross underneath the Indian Caucasus,[1]
That vast sky-neighboring mountain of milk snow;
Crossing so high, that, as they mount, they pass
Long flocks of traveling birds dead on the snow,
Choked by the air, and scarce can they themselves   165
Slake their parch'd throats with sugar'd mulberries —
In single file they move, and stop their breath,
For fear they should dislodge the o'erhanging snows —
So the pale Persians held their breath with fear.
And to Ferood his brother chiefs came up   170
To counsel; Gudurz and Zoarrah[2] came,
And Feraburz, who ruled the Persian host
Second, and was the uncle of the King;
These came and counsel'd, and then Gudurz said : —
"Ferood, shame bids us take their challenge up,   175
Yet champion have we none to match this youth.
He has the wild stag's foot, the lion's heart.[3]
But Rustum came last night; aloof he sits
And sullen, and has pitch'd his tents apart.
Him will I seek, and carry to his ear   180
The Tartar challenge, and this young man's name.
Haply he will forget his wrath, and fight.
Stand forth the while, and take their challenge up."
So spake he ; and Ferood stood forth and cried : —
"Old man, be it agreed as thou hast said !   185
Let Sohrab arm, and we will find a man."
He spake : and Peran-Wisa turn'd, and strode

---

[1] One of the names of the Hindu Koosh Mountains, the lofty range which separates Afghanistan from Turkistan.   [2] Zō-är'äh.

[3] "The wild stag's foot," etc., i.e., the endurance and activity of the wild stag, the courage of the lion.

Back through the opening squadrons to his tent.
But through the anxious Persians Gudurz ran,
190 And cross'd the camp which lay behind, and reach'd,
Out on the sands beyond it, Rustum's tents.
Of scarlet cloth they were, and glittering gay,
Just pitch'd; the high pavilion in the midst
Was Rustum's, and his men lay camp'd around.
195 And Gudurz enter'd Rustum's tent, and found
Rustum; his morning meal was done, but still
The table stood before him, charged with food —
A side of roasted sheep, and cakes of bread,
And dark-green melons; and there Rustum sate [1]
200 Listless, and held a falcon [2] on his wrist,
And play'd with it; but Gudurz came and stood
Before him; and he look'd, and saw him stand,
And with a cry sprang up and dropp'd the bird,
And greeted Gudurz with both hands, and said: —
205   "Welcome! these eyes could see no better sight.
What news? but sit down first, and eat and drink."
But Gudurz stood in the tent door, and said: —
"Not now! a time will come to eat and drink,
But not to-day; to-day has other needs.
210 The armies are drawn out, and stand at gaze;
For from the Tartars is a challenge brought
To pick a champion from the Persian lords
To fight their champion — and thou know'st his name —
Sohrab men call him, but his birth is hid.
215 O Rustum, like thy might is this young man's!
He has the wild stag's foot, the lion's heart;
And he is young, and Iran's chiefs are old,
Or else too weak; and all eyes turn to thee.
Come down and help us, Rustum, or we lose!"

[1] Old form of "sat."
[2] Falconry was known in Asia as early as 1700 B.C., and to the present day has been a favorite sport in that country.

He spoke; but Rustum answer'd with a smile: —   220
" Go to ! if Iran's chiefs are old, then I
Am older; if the young are weak, the King
Errs strangely; for the King, for Kai Khosroo,[1]
Himself is young, and honors younger men,
And lets the aged molder to their graves.   225
Rustum he loves no more, but loves the young —
The young may rise at Sohrab's vaunts, not I.
For what care I, though all speak Sohrab's fame ?
For would that I myself had such a son,
And not that one slight helpless girl [2] I have —   230
A son so famed, so brave, to send to war,
And I to tarry with the snow-hair'd Zal,[3]
My father, whom the robber Afghans vex,
And clip his borders short, and drive his herds,
And he has none to guard his weak old age.   235
There would I go, and hang my armor up,
And with my great name fence that weak old man,
And spend the goodly treasures I have got,
And rest my age, and hear of Sohrab's fame,
And leave to death the hosts of thankless kings,   240
And with these slaughterous hands draw sword no more."
      He spoke, and smiled; and Gudurz made reply: —
" What then, O Rustum, will men say to this,
When Sohrab dares our bravest forth, and seeks

---

[1] Kī Kŏs-roo', the third King of Persia of the dynasty called Kaianides.
He succeeded his grandfather Kai Kä'oos in the sixth century B.C. The Shah
Nameh places the episode of Sohrab and Rustum in the reign of the latter
monarch.

[2] See p. 35, lines 609–611; also Introduction, p. 10.

[3] It is related in the Shah Nameh that Zal was born with snow-white hair,—
a monstrosity which so shocked his father Säm, that the latter abandoned the
babe on the heights of the Elburz Mountains. Zal was miraculously pre-
served, however, by a great bird, or griffin, and reclaimed by his repentant
parent. He subsequently married the Princess Rudä'beh of Zabulistan
(Seistan), and became the father of Rustum.

245 Thee most of all, and thou, whom most he seeks,
    Hidest thy face ?   Take heed lest men should say :
    ' Like some old miser, Rustum hoards his fame,
    And shuns to peril it with younger men.' "
        And, greatly moved, then Rustum made reply : —
250 " O Gudurz, wherefore dost thou say such words ?
    Thou knowest better words than this to say.
    What is one more, one less, obscure or famed,
    Valiant or craven, young or old, to me ?
    Are not they mortal, am not I myself ?
255 But who for men of naught would do great deeds ?
    Come, thou shalt see how Rustum hoards his fame !
    But I will fight unknown, and in plain arms ;
    Let not men say of Rustum, he was match'd
    In single fight with any mortal man."
260   He spoke, and frown'd ; and Gudurz turn'd, and ran
    Back quickly through the camp in fear and joy —
    Fear at his wrath, but joy that Rustum came.
    But Rustum strode to his tent door, and call'd
    His followers in, and bade them bring his arms,
265 And clad himself in steel ; the arms he chose
    Were plain, and on his shield was no device,
    Only his helm was rich, inlaid with gold,
    And, from the fluted spine atop, a plume
    Of horsehair waved, a scarlet horsehair plume.
270 So arm'd, he issued forth ; and Ruksh, his horse,
    Follow'd him like a faithful hound at heel —
    Ruksh, whose renown was noised through all the earth,
    The horse, whom Rustum on a foray once
    Did in Bokhara by the river find
275 A colt beneath its dam, and drove him home,
    And rear'd him ; a bright bay, with lofty crest,
    Dight [1] with a saddlecloth of broider'd green

---

[1] Dressed.

Crusted with gold, and on the ground were work'd
All beasts of chase, all beasts which hunters know.
So follow'd, Rustum left his tents, and cross'd   280
The camp, and to the Persian host appear'd.
And all the Persians knew him, and with shouts
Hail'd; but the Tartars knew not who he was.
And dear as the wet diver to the eyes
Of his pale wife who waits and weeps on shore,   285
By sandy Bahrein,[1] in the Persian Gulf,
Plunging all day in the blue waves, at night,
Having made up his tale[2] of precious pearls,
Rejoins her in their hut upon the sands —
So dear to the pale Persians Rustum came.   290
   And Rustum to the Persian front advanced,
And Sohrab arm'd in Haman's tent, and came.
And as afield the reapers cut a swath
Down through the middle of a rich man's corn,
And on each side are squares of standing corn,   295
And in the midst a stubble, short and bare —
So on each side were squares of men, with spears
Bristling, and in the midst, the open sand.
And Rustum came upon the sand, and cast
His eyes toward the Tartar tents, and saw   300
Sohrab come forth, and eyed him as he came.
   As some rich woman, on a winter's morn,
Eyes through her silken curtains the poor drudge
Who with numb blacken'd fingers makes her fire —
At cock-crow, on a starlit winter's morn,   305
When the frost flowers[3] the whiten'd windowpanes —
And wonders how she lives, and what the thoughts
Of that poor drudge may be; so Rustum eyed

---

[1] Bahrein (bäh'rān), or Mä-nä'mä, is an island in the Persian Gulf, famous for its pearl fisheries.
[2] Count or reckoning.
[3] Decorates.

The unknown adventurous youth, who from afar
310 Came seeking Rustum, and defying forth
All the most valiant chiefs; long he perused
His spirited air, and wonder'd who he was.
For very young he seem'd, tenderly rear'd;
Like some young cypress, tall, and dark, and straight,
315 Which in a queen's secluded garden throws
Its slight dark shadow on the moonlit turf,
By midnight, to a bubbling fountain's sound—
So slender Sohrab seem'd, so softly rear'd.
And a deep pity enter'd Rustum's soul
320 As he beheld him coming; and he stood,
And beckon'd to him with his hand, and said:—
"O thou young man, the air of heaven is soft,
And warm, and pleasant; but the grave is cold!
Heaven's air is better than the cold dead grave.
325 Behold me! I am vast,[1] and clad in iron,
And tried;[2] and I have stood on many a field
Of blood, and I have fought with many a foe—
Never was that field lost, or that foe saved.
O Sohrab, wherefore wilt thou rush on death?
330 Be govern'd![3] quit the Tartar host, and come
To Iran, and be as my son to me,
And fight beneath my banner till I die!
There are no youths in Iran brave as thou."
So he spake, mildly; Sohrab heard his voice,
335 The mighty voice of Rustum, and he saw
His giant figure planted on the sand,
Sole, like some single tower, which a chief
Hath builded on the waste in former years
Against the robbers; and he saw that head,
340 Streak'd with its first gray hairs;—hope fill'd his soul,
And he ran forward and embraced his knees,

---

[1] Mighty.   [2] Experienced.   [3] Advised.

And clasp'd his hand within his own, and said : —
" Oh, by thy father's head ! by thine own soul !
Art thou not Rustum ? speak ! art thou not he ? "
But Rustum eyed askance the kneeling youth,   345
And turn'd away, and spake to his own soul : —
" Ah me, I muse what this young fox may mean !
False, wily, boastful, are these Tartar boys.
For if I now confess this thing he asks,
And hide it not, but say : ' Rustum is here ! '   350
He will not yield indeed, nor quit our foes,
But he will find some pretext not to fight,
And praise my fame, and proffer courteous gifts,
A belt or sword perhaps, and go his way.
And on a feast tide, in Afrasiab's hall,   355
In Samarcand, he will arise and cry :
' I challenged once, when the two armies camp'd
Beside the Oxus, all the Persian lords
To cope with me in single fight ; but they
Shrank, only Rustum dared ; then he and I   360
Changed gifts, and went on equal terms away.'
So will he speak, perhaps, while men applaud ;
Then were the chiefs of Iran shamed through me."
     And then he turn'd, and sternly spake aloud : —
" Rise ! wherefore dost thou vainly question thus   365
Of Rustum ?   I am here, whom thou hast call'd
By challenge forth ; make good thy vaunt, or yield !
Is it with Rustum only thou wouldst fight ?
Rash boy, men look on Rustum's face and flee !
For well I know, that did great Rustum stand   370
Before thy face this day, and were reveal'd,
There would be then no talk of fighting more.
But being what I am, I tell thee this —
Do thou record it in thine inmost soul :
Either thou shalt renounce thy vaunt and yield,   375
Or else thy bones shall strew this sand, till winds

Bleach them, or Oxus with his summer floods,
Oxus in summer wash them all away."
  He spoke; and Sohrab answer'd, on his feet: —
380 " Art thou so fierce ? Thou wilt not fright me so !
I am no girl, to be made pale by words.
Yet this thou hast said well, did Rustum stand
Here on this field, there were no fighting then.
But Rustum is far hence, and we stand here.
385 Begin ! thou art more vast, more dread than I,
And thou art proved, I know, and I am young —
But yet success sways with the breath of heaven.
And though thou thinkest that thou knowest sure
Thy victory, yet thou canst not surely know.
390 For we are all, like swimmers in the sea,
Poised on the top of a huge wave of fate,
Which hangs uncertain to which side to fall.
And whether it will heave us up to land,
Or whether it will roll us out to sea,
395 Back out to sea, to the deep waves of death,
We know not, and no search will make us know;
Only the event will teach us in its hour."
  He spoke, and Rustum answer'd not, but hurl'd
His spear; down from the shoulder, down it came,
400 As on some partridge in the corn a hawk,
That long has tower'd in the airy clouds,
Drops like a plummet; Sohrab saw it come,
And sprang aside, quick as a flash; the spear
Hiss'd, and went quivering down into the sand,
405 Which it sent flying wide; — then Sohrab threw
In turn, and full struck Rustum's shield; sharp rang,
The iron plates rang sharp, but turn'd the spear.
And Rustum seized his club, which none but he
Could wield; an unlopp'd trunk it was, and huge,
410 Still rough — like those which men in treeless plains
To build them boats fish from the flooded rivers,

Hyphasis or Hydaspes,[1] when, high up
By their dark springs, the wind in winter time
Hath made in Himalayan forests wrack,[2]
And strewn the channels with torn boughs — so huge 415
The club which Rustum lifted now, and struck
One stroke; but again Sohrab sprang aside,
Lithe as the glancing snake, and the club came
Thundering to earth, and leapt from Rustum's hand.
And Rustum follow'd his own blow, and fell   420
To his knees, and with his fingers clutch'd the sand;
And now might Sohrab have unsheathed his sword,
And pierced the mighty Rustum while he lay
Dizzy, and on his knees, and choked with sand;
But he look'd on, and smiled, nor bared his sword, 425
But courteously drew back, and spoke, and said: —
    "Thou strik'st too hard! that club of thine will float
Upon the summer floods, and not my bones.
But rise, and be not wroth! not wroth am I;
No, when I see thee, wrath forsakes my soul.   430
Thou say'st, thou art not Rustum; be it so!
Who art thou then, that canst so touch my soul?
Boy as I am, I have seen battles too —
Have waded foremost in their bloody waves,
And heard their hollow roar of dying men;   435
But never was my heart thus touch'd before.
Are they from Heaven, these softenings of the heart?
O thou old warrior, let us yield to Heaven!
Come, plant we here in earth our angry spears,
And make a truce, and sit upon this sand,   440
And pledge each other in red wine, like friends,
And thou shalt talk to me of Rustum's deeds.
There are enough foes in the Persian host,

---

[1] Hyphasis, Hydaspes, are the ancient names of the Beas and the Jhylum,
— two of the great rivers of the Indus system in the Punjab of northern India.
[2] Wreck, or ruin.

Whom I may meet, and strike, and feel no pang;
445   Champions enough Afrasiab has, whom thou
Mayst fight; fight *them*, when they confront thy spear!
But oh, let there be peace 'twixt thee and me!"
He ceased, but while he spake, Rustum had risen,
And stood erect, trembling with rage; his club
450   He left to lie, but had regain'd his spear,
Whose fiery point now in his mail'd right hand
Blazed bright and baleful, like that autumn star,[1]
The baleful sign of fevers; dust had soil'd
His stately crest, and dimm'd his glittering arms.
455   His breast heaved, his lips foam'd, and twice his voice
Was choked with rage; at last these words broke way: —
"Girl! nimble with thy feet, not with thy hands!
Curl'd minion, dancer, coiner of sweet words!
Fight, let me hear thy hateful voice no more!
460   Thou art not in Afrasiab's gardens now
With Tartar girls, with whom thou art wont to dance;
But on the Oxus sands, and in the dance
Of battle, and with me, who make no play
Of war; I fight it out, and hand to hand.
465   Speak not to me of truce, and pledge, and wine!
Remember all thy valor; try thy feints
And cunning! all the pity I had is gone;
Because thou hast shamed me before both the hosts
With thy light skipping tricks, and thy girl's wiles."
470   He spoke, and Sohrab kindled at his taunts,
And he too drew his sword; at once they rush'd
Together, as two eagles on one prey
Come rushing down together from the clouds,
One from the east, one from the west; their shields

[1] It was the belief, not only of the ancient races, but of some comparatively modern writers, that there is a close connection between certain planets and the prevalence of epidemic diseases. The star referred to is probably Sirius, the Dog Star.

Dash'd with a clang together, and a din 475
Rose, such as that the sinewy woodcutters
Make often in the forest's heart at morn,
Of hewing axes, crashing trees — such blows
Rustum and Sohrab on each other hail'd.
And you would say that sun and stars took part 480
In that unnatural[1] conflict; for a cloud
Grew suddenly in heaven, and dark'd the sun
Over the fighters' heads; and a wind rose
Under their feet, and moaning swept the plain,
And in a sandy whirlwind wrapp'd the pair. 485
In gloom they twain were wrapp'd, and they alone;
For both the on-looking hosts on either hand
Stood in broad daylight, and the sky was pure,
And the sun sparkled on the Oxus stream.
But in the gloom they fought, with bloodshot eyes 490
And laboring breath; first Rustum struck the shield
Which Sohrab held stiff out; the steel-spiked spear
Rent the tough plates, but fail'd to reach the skin,
And Rustum pluck'd it back with angry groan.
Then Sohrab with his sword smote Rustum's helm, 495
Nor clove its steel quite through; but all the crest
He shore[2] away, and that proud horsehair plume,
Never till now defiled, sank to the dust;
And Rustum bow'd his head; but then the gloom
Grew blacker, thunder rumbled in the air, 500
And lightnings rent the cloud; and Ruksh, the horse,
Who stood at hand, utter'd a dreadful cry; —
No horse's cry was that, most like the roar
Of some pain'd desert lion, who all day
Hath trail'd the hunter's javelin in his side, 505
And comes at night to die upon the sand.

---

[1] Unnatural because between father and son.
[2] Past tense of "shear" ("to cut").

The two hosts heard that cry, and quaked for fear,
And Oxus curdled [1] as it cross'd his stream.
But Sohrab heard, and quail'd not, but rush'd on,
510   And struck again; and again Rustum bow'd
His head; but this time all the blade, like glass,
Sprang in a thousand shivers on the helm,
And in the hand the hilt remain'd alone.
Then Rustum raised his head; his dreadful eyes
515   Glared, and he shook on high his menacing spear,
And shouted: "Rustum!"—Sohrab heard that shout,
And shrank amazed: back he recoil'd one step,
And scann'd with blinking eyes the advancing form;
And then he stood bewilder'd, and he dropp'd
520   His covering shield, and the spear pierced his side.
He reel'd, and, staggering back, sank to the ground;
And then the gloom dispersed, and the wind fell,
And the bright sun broke forth, and melted all
The cloud; and the two armies saw the pair—
525   Saw Rustum standing, safe upon his feet,
And Sohrab, wounded, on the bloody sand.
     Then, with a bitter smile, Rustum began:—
"Sohrab, thou thoughtest in thy mind to kill
A Persian lord this day, and strip his corpse,
530   And bear thy trophies to Afrasiab's tent;
Or else that the great Rustum would come down
Himself to fight, and that thy wiles would move
His heart to take a gift, and let thee go;
And then that all the Tartar host would praise
535   Thy courage or thy craft, and spread thy fame,
To glad thy father in his weak old age.
Fool, thou art slain, and by an unknown man!
Dearer to the red jackals shalt thou be
Than to thy friends, and to thy father old."

1 Thickened with fear.

And, with a fearless mien, Sohrab replied : — 540
" Unknown thou art; yet thy fierce vaunt is vain.
Thou dost not slay me, proud and boastful man !
No ! Rustum slays me, and this filial heart.
For were I .match'd with ten such men as thee,
And I were that which till to-day I was, 545
They should be lying here, I standing there.
But that beloved name unnerved my arm —
That name, and something, I confess, in thee,
Which troubles all my heart, and made my shield
Fall; and thy spear transfix'd an unarm'd foe. 550
And now thou boastest, and insult'st my fate.
But hear thou this, fierce man, tremble to hear:
The mighty Rustum shall avenge my death !
My father, whom I seek through all the world,
He shall avenge my death, and punish thee !" 555
   As when some hunter in the spring hath found
A breeding eagle sitting on her nest,
Upon the craggy isle of a hill lake,
And pierced her with an arrow as she rose,
And follow'd her to find her where she fell 560
Far off; — anon her mate comes winging back
From hunting, and a great way off descries
His huddling young left sole; [1] at that, he checks
His pinion, and with short uneasy sweeps
Circles above his eyry, with loud screams 565
Chiding his mate back to her nest; but she
Lies dying, with the arrow in her side,
In some far stony gorge out of his ken,
A heap of fluttering feathers — never more
Shall the lake glass [2] her, flying over it; 570
Never the black and dripping precipices
Echo her stormy scream as she sails by —

---

[1] Solitary, alone.   [2] Reflect, as in a mirror.

3

As that poor bird flies home, nor knows his loss,
So Rustum knew not his own loss, but stood
575   Over his dying son, and knew him not.
        But, with a cold incredulous voice, he said : —
" What prate is this of fathers and revenge ?
The mighty Rustum never had a son."
        And, with a failing voice, Sohrab replied : —
580   " Ah yes, he had ! and that lost son am I.
Surely the news will one day reach his ear,
Reach Rustum, where he sits, and tarries long,
Somewhere, I know not where, but far from here ;
And pierce him like a stab, and make him leap
585   To arms, and cry for vengeance upon thee.
Fierce man, bethink thee, for an only son !
What will that grief, what will that vengeance be ?
Oh, could I live till I that grief had seen !
Yet him I pity not so much, but her,
590   My mother, who in Ader-baijan dwells
With that old king, her father, who grows gray
With age, and rules over the valiant Koords.
Her most I pity, who no more will see
Sohrab returning from the Tartar camp,
595   With spoils and honor, when the war is done.
  ·   But a dark rumor will be bruited up,[1]
From tribe to tribe, until it reach her ear ;
And then will that defenseless woman learn
That Sohrab will rejoice her sight no more,
600   But that in battle with a nameless foe,
By the far-distant Oxus, he is slain."
        He spoke ; and as he ceased, he wept aloud,
Thinking of her he left, and his own death.
He spoke ; but Rustum listen'd, plunged in thought.
605   Nor did he yet believe it was his son

---

[1] " Bruited up," i.e., noised abroad.

Who spoke, although he call'd back names he knew;
For he had had sure tidings that the babe,
Which was in Ader-baijan born to him,
Had been a puny girl, no boy at all —
So that sad mother sent him word, for fear   610
Rustum should seek the boy, to train in arms.
And so he deem'd that either Sohrab took,
By a false boast, the style [1] of Rustum's son;
Or that men gave it him, to swell his fame.
So deem'd he: yet he listen'd, plunged in thought; 615
And his soul set to grief, as the vast tide
Of the bright rocking Ocean sets to shore
At the full moon; tears gather'd in his eyes;
For he remember'd his own early youth,
And all its bounding rapture; as, at dawn,   620
The shepherd from his mountain lodge descries
A far, bright city, smitten by the sun,
Through many rolling clouds — so Rustum saw
His youth; saw Sohrab's mother, in her bloom;
And that old king,[2] her father, who loved well   625
His wandering guest, and gave him his fair child
With joy; and all the pleasant life they led,
They three, in that long-distant summer time —
The castle, and the dewy woods, and hunt
And hound, and morn on those delightful hills   630
In Ader-baijan. And he saw that youth,
Of age and looks to be his own dear son,[3]
Piteous and lovely, lying on the sand,
Like some rich hyacinth which by the scythe
Of an unskillful gardener has been cut,   635
Mowing the garden grassplots near its bed,
And lies, a fragrant tower of purple bloom,

[1] Title or name.   See Introduction, p. 10.
[3] "Of age," etc., of such age and looks that he might have been his son.

On the mown, dying grass — so Sohrab lay,
Lovely in death, upon the common sand.
640   And Rustum gazed on him with grief, and said :—
"O Sohrab, thou indeed art such a son
Whom Rustum, wert thou his, might well have loved !
Yet here thou errest, Sohrab, or else men
Have told thee false — thou art not Rustum's son.
645   For Rustum had no son; one child he had —
But one — a girl; who with her mother now
Plies some light female task, nor dreams of us —
Of us she dreams not, nor of wounds, nor war."
     But Sohrab answer'd him in wrath; for now
650   The anguish of the deep-fix'd spear grew fierce,
And he desired to draw forth the steel,
And let the blood flow free, and so to die —
But first he would convince his stubborn foe;
And, rising sternly on one arm, he said :—
655   "Man, who art thou who dost deny my words ?
Truth sits upon the lips of dying men,
And falsehood, while I lived, was far from mine.
I tell thee, prick'd upon this arm I bear
That seal which Rustum to my mother gave,
660   That she might prick it on the babe she bore."
     He spoke; and all the blood left Rustum's cheeks,
And his knees totter'd, and he smote his hand
Against his breast, his heavy mailed hand,
That the hard iron corselet clank'd aloud;
665   And to his heart he press'd the other hand,
And in a hollow voice he spake, and said : —
     "Sohrab, that were a proof which could not lie !
If thou show this, then art thou Rustum's son."
     Then, with weak hasty fingers, Sohrab loosed
670   His belt, and near the shoulder bared his arm,
And show'd a sign in faint vermilion points
Prick'd; as a cunning workman, in Pekin,

Pricks with vermilion some clear porcelain vase,
An emperor's gift — at early morn he paints,
And all day long, and, when night comes, the lamp 675
Lights up his studious forehead and thin hands —
So delicately prick'd the sign appear'd
On Sohrab's arm, the sign of Rustum's seal.
It was that griffin,[1] which of old rear'd Zal,
Rustum's great father, whom they left to die, 680
A helpless babe, among the mountain rocks;
Him that kind creature found, and rear'd and loved —
Then Rustum took it for his glorious sign.
And Sohrab bared that image on his arm,
And himself scann'd it long with mournful eyes, 685
And then he touch'd it with his hand, and said: —
"How say'st thou? Is that sign the proper sign
Of Rustum's son, or of some other man's?"
He spoke; but Rustum gazed, and gazed, and stood
Speechless; and then he utter'd one sharp cry: 690
"O boy — thy father!" — and his voice choked there.
And then a dark cloud pass'd before his eyes,
And his head swam, and he sank down to earth.
But Sohrab crawl'd to where he lay, and cast
His arms about his neck, and kiss'd his lips, 695
And with fond faltering fingers stroked his cheeks,
Trying to call him back to life; and life
Came back to Rustum, and he oped his eyes,
And they stood wide with horror; and he seized
In both his hands the dust which lay around, 700
And threw it on his head, and smirch'd his hair, —
His hair, and face, and beard, and glittering arms;
And strong convulsive groanings shook his breast,
And his sobs choked him; and he clutch'd his sword,
To draw it, and forever let life out. 705

1 See Note 3, p. 23.

But Sohrab saw his thought, and held his hands,
And with a soothing voice he spake, and said : —
"Father, forbear ! for I but meet to-day
The doom which at my birth was written down
710 In heaven, and thou art heaven's unconscious hand.
Surely my heart cried out that it was thou,
When first I saw thee ; and thy heart spoke too,
I know it ! but fate trod those promptings down
Under its iron heel ; fate, fate engaged
715 The strife, and hurl'd me on my father's spear.
But let us speak no more of this ! I find
My father ; let me feel that I have found !
Come, sit beside me on this sand, and take
My head betwixt thy hands, and kiss my cheeks,
720 And wash them with thy tears, and say : 'My son !'
Quick ! quick ! for number'd are my sands of life,
And swift ; for like the lightning to this field
I came, and like the wind I go away —
Sudden, and swift, and like a passing wind.
725 But it was writ in heaven that this should be."
So said he, and his voice released the heart
Of Rustum, and his tears broke forth ; he cast
His arms round his son's neck, and wept aloud,
And kiss'd him. And awe fell on both the hosts,
730 When they saw Rustum's grief ; and Ruksh, the horse,
With his head bowing to the ground and mane
Sweeping the dust, came near, and in mute woe
First to the one then to the other moved
His head, as if inquiring what their grief
735 Might mean ; and from his dark, compassionate eyes,
The big warm tears roll'd down, and caked[1] the sand.
But Rustum chid him with stern voice, and said : —
"Ruksh, now thou grievest ; but, O Ruksh, thy feet
Should first have rotted on their nimble joints,

[1] Hardened or formed into cakes.

Or ere they brought thy master to this field !" 740
  But Sohrab look'd upon the horse, and said: —
"Is this, then, Ruksh ?　How often, in past days,
My mother told me of thee, thou brave steed,
My terrible father's terrible horse ! and said,
That I should one day find thy lord and thee. 745
Come, let me lay my hand upon thy mane !
O Ruksh, thou art more fortunate than I ;
For thou hast gone where I shall never go,
And snuff'd the breezes of my father's home.
And thou hast trod the sands of Seistan, 750
And seen the River of Helmund, and the Lake
Of Zirrah ; [1] and the aged Zal himself
Has often stroked thy neck, and given thee food,
Corn in a golden platter soak'd with wine,
And said: 'O Ruksh ! bear Rustum well,' — but I 755
Have never known my grandsire's furrow'd face,
Nor seen his lofty house in Seistan,
Nor slaked my thirst at the clear Helmund stream ;
But lodged among my father's foes, and seen
Afrasiab's cities only, Samarcand, 760
Bokhara, and lone Khiva in the waste,
And the black Toorkmun tents ; and only drunk
The desert rivers, Moorghab and Tejend,
Kohik, and where the Kalmuks feed their sheep,
The northern Sir ; [2] and this great Oxus stream, 765
The yellow Oxus, by whose brink I die."
  Then, with a heavy groan, Rustum bewail'd : —
"Oh, that its waves were flowing over me !
Oh, that I saw its grains of yellow silt
Roll tumbling in the current o'er my head !" 770

[1] See Note 1, p. 18.
[2] The Moorghab, Tejend (Tedzend), and Kohik are rivers of Turkistan
which lose themselves in the desert south of Bokhara.　The " northern Sir "
is the Syr Daria, or Jaxartes.

But, with a grave mild voice, Sohrab replied : —
"Desire not that, my father ! thou must live.
For some are born to do great deeds, and live,
As some are born to be obscured, and die.
775   Do thou the deeds I die too young to do,
And reap a second glory in thine age ;
Thou art my father, and thy gain is mine.
But come ! thou seest this great host of men
Which follow me ; I pray thee, slay not these!
780   Let me entreat for them ; what have they done ?
They follow'd me, my hope, my fame, my star.
Let them all cross the Oxus back in peace.
But me thou must bear hence, not send with them,
But carry me with thee to Seistan,
785   And place me on a bed, and mourn for me,
Thou, and the snow-hair'd Zal, and all thy friends.
And thou must lay me in that lovely earth,
And heap a stately mound above my bones,
And plant a far-seen pillar over all.
790   That so the passing horseman on the waste
May see my tomb a great way off, and cry :
'Sohrab, the mighty Rustum's son, lies there,
Whom his great father did in ignorance kill !'
And I be not forgotten in my grave."
795   And, with a mournful voice, Rustum replied : —
"Fear not ! as thou hast said, Sohrab, my son,
So shall it be ; for I will burn my tents,
And quit the host, and bear thee hence with me,
And carry thee away to Seistan,
800   And place thee on a bed, and mourn for thee,
With the snow-headed Zal, and all my friends.
And I will lay thee in that lovely earth,
And heap a stately mound above thy bones,
And plant a far-seen pillar over all,
805   And men shall not forget thee in thy grave.

And I will spare thy host; yea, let them go !
Let them all cross the Oxus back in peace !
What should I do with slaying any more ?
For would that all that I have ever slain
Might be once more alive; my bitterest foes,   810
And they who were call'd champions in their time,
And through whose death I won that fame I have —
And I were nothing but a common man,
A poor, mean soldier, and without renown,
So thou mightest live too, my son, my son !   815
Or rather would that I, even I myself,
Might now be lying on this bloody sand,
Near death, and by an ignorant stroke of thine,
Not thou of mine ! and I might die, not thou;
And I, not thou, be borne to Seistan;   820
And Zal might weep above my grave, not thine;
And say : ' O son, I weep thee not too sore,
For willingly, I know, thou met'st thine end !'
But now in blood and battles was my youth,
And full of blood and battles is my age,   825
And I shall never end this life of blood."
    Then, at the point of death, Sohrab replied : —
" A life of blood indeed, thou dreadful man !
But thou shalt yet have peace; only not now,
Not yet ! but thou shalt have it on that day [1]   830
When thou shalt sail in a high-masted ship,

[1] Soon after the death of Afrasiab, against whom Kai Khosroo had waged
a ceaseless warfare, the Persian monarch determined to spend the rest of his
life in religious retirement. He divided his dominions among his nobles, and
then, accompanied by some of them, he went to a spring which had been
fixed upon as the place of his repose. There he disappeared suddenly and
mysteriously " in the twinkling of an eye;" and all those who went with
him were destroyed on the return voyage by a violent tempest. According
to Sohrab's prophecy, we would suppose Rustum to have been among those
peers who accompanied Kai Khosroo; yet, according to the Shah Nameh,
he was not among those who perished.

Thou and the other peers of Kai Khosroo,
Returning home over the salt blue sea,
From laying thy dear master in his grave."
835   And Rustum gazed in Sohrab's face, and said:—
"Soon be that day, my son, and deep that sea !
Till then, if fate so wills, let me endure."
He spoke; and Sohrab smiled on him, and took
The spear, and drew it from his side, and eased
840   His wound's imperious anguish; but the blood
Came welling from the open gash, and life
Flow'd with the stream; — all down his cold white side
The crimson torrent ran, dim now and soil'd,
Like the soil'd tissue of white violets
845   Left, freshly gather'd, on their native bank,
By children whom their nurses call with haste
Indoors from the sun's eye; his head droop'd low,
His limbs grew slack; motionless, white, he lay —
White, with eyes closed; only when heavy gasps,
850   Deep heavy gasps quivering through all his frame,
Convulsed him back to life, he open'd them,
And fix'd them feebly on his father's face;
Till now all strength was ebb'd, and from his limbs
Unwillingly the spirit fled away,
855   Regretting the warm mansion which it left,
And youth, and bloom, and this delightful world.
So, on the bloody sand, Sohrab lay dead;
And the great Rustum drew his horseman's cloak
Down o'er his face, and sate by his dead son.
860   As those black granite pillars, once high-rear'd
By Jemshid in Persepolis,[1] to bear

---

[1] An ancient city of Persia.   On its site are found the ruins of enormous buildings, and conspicuous among them, the huge black granite pillars, some of which are still standing.   These remains go by the name of " Takhti Jamshid," which translated is " the throne of Jamshid or Jemshid," a mythical king.

His house, now 'mid their broken flights of steps
Lie prone, enormous, down the mountain side —
So in the sand lay Rustum by his son.
And night came down' over the solemn waste,   865
And the two gazing hosts, and that sole pair,
And darken'd all; and a cold fog, with night,
Crept from the Oxus. Soon a hum arose,
As of a great assembly loosed, and fires
Began to twinkle through the fog; for now   870
Both armies moved to camp, and took their meal;
The Persians took it on the open sands
Southward, the Tartars by the river marge;
And Rustum and his son were left alone.

But the majestic river floated on,   875
Out of the mist and hum of that low land,
Into the frosty starlight, and there moved,
Rejoicing, through the hush'd Chorasmian [1] waste,
Under the solitary moon; — he flow'd
Right for the polar star, past Orgunjè,[2]   880
Brimming, and bright, and large; then sands begin
To hem his watery march, and dam his streams,
And split his currents; that for many a league
The shorn and parcel'd Oxus strains along
Through beds of sand and matted rushy isles —   885
Oxus, forgetting the bright speed he had
In his high mountain cradle in Pamere,
A foil'd circuitous wanderer — till at last
The long'd-for dash of waves is heard, and wide

---

[1] Chorasmia is the ancient name of Kharasm, or Karissim, — a region of Turkistan on the Oxus, and at one time the seat of a powerful empire. Its present limits seem to be about those of Khiva.

[2] Oor-ghěnj', a village on the Oxus about 70 miles below Khiva, and near the head of its delta.

890   His luminous home [1] of waters opens, bright
     And tranquil, from whose floor the new-bathed [2] stars
     Emerge, and shine upon the Aral Sea.

[1] The Aral Sea.

[2] The horizon is the point where earth and sky, or sky and water, seem to meet: hence the stars, when they appear above the horizon, seem to emerge from the sea.

www.ingramcontent.com/pod-product-compliance
Lightning Source LLC
Chambersburg PA
CBHW031617040426
42452CB00006B/569